THE WHITE HOUSE
The Home of the President of the United States

By Steven Thomsen

PUBLISHED BY

Capstone Press

Mankato, MN, U.S.A.

Distributed By

⊄P CHILDRENS PRESS ®

CHICAGO

CIP
LIBRARY OF CONGRESS CATALOGING IN PUBLICATION DATA

Thomsen, Steven.
The White House / by Steven Thomsen.
p. cm.--(Inside story)
Summary: Traces the historical development of the home of the presidents
of the United States, describes past and present rooms, and recounts
memorable events that took place there during selected administrations.
ISBN 1-56065-025-7
1. White House (Washington, D.C.)--Juvenile literature.
2. Washington (D.C.)--Buildings, structures, etc.--Juvenile literature.
3. Presidents--United States--History--Juvenile literature. [1. White House
(Washington, D.C.) 2. Washington (D.C.)--Buildings, structures, etc. 3.
Presidents.] I. Title. II. Series: Inside story (Mankato, Minn.)
F204.W5T46 1989
975.3--dc20   89-25166 CIP AC

PHOTO CREDITS

The White House (Susan Biddle): 12
Jimmy Carter Library: 4, 21, 22, 29, 32-33, 35, 36, 39, 40, 42-43

Designed by Nathan Y. Jarvis & Associates, Inc.

Capstone Press
Box 669, Mankato, MN, U.S A. 56001

CONTENTS

INTRODUCTION

"Did you get to see the president?" Jenny called out to her father as he walked in the front door. Her father had just returned from a trip to Washington, D.C.

"No," he said with a chuckle. "But I did get to see his house."

While in our nation's capital, Jenny's father had driven down the broad boulevards. He had seen the National Zoo, the Lincoln Memorial, and the United States Capitol Building. His trip down Pennsylvania Avenue took him right past the White House, the home of the U.S. President.

"It's really a magnificent sight," he said. "It's surrounded by a park and beautiful lawns and trees. It's not far from the Potomac River.

"Just before my plane landed, it flew over much of the city. I could see so many wonderful sights. In the distance, I could see the White House glistening in the sunlight," he said.

Jenny's father reached into his suitcase. To Jenny's surprise, he pulled out a large present wrapped in colorful paper. Jenny tore off the bow and removed the wrapping paper. It was a picture book full of photographs of Washington, D.C. Some of the photographs were very old. The book told the story of our nation's capital and the White House.

She quickly turned the pages. Soon, she came to a large photograph of the White House. "I wonder what it would be like to live there," she thought.

THE BIRTH OF A GRAND CITY

It had rained for several days. It was early March in the Maryland and Virginia countryside. Spring still had not arrived. In between the heavy rains and thunderstorms, a chilly fog had moved in to cover the distant tobacco fields. As far as the eye could see were marshes and rolling hills.

Major Pierre Charles L'Enfant quietly stood beside his horse and gazed across the misty scene. He tried to imagine how the "Federal City" would be built. The year was 1792.

In the distance L'Enfant could see only a few wooden farmhouses. Nearby flowed the Potomac and the Eastern Branch (now the Anacostia River). On the Virginia side was

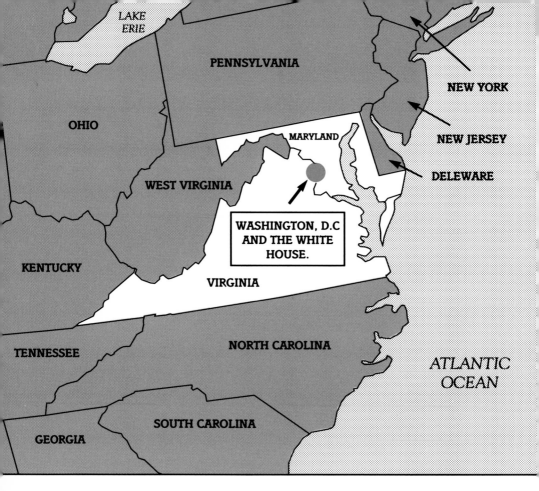

Washington, D.C., and the location of the White House.

the port town of Alexandria. That town had been laid out by George Washington's brother, Lawrence, when he was only 17. To the west, on the Maryland side, was another tobacco port named after King George II of England. It eventually became known as Georgetown.

8

In far-away New York, George Washington dreamed of a new city for the headquarters of the young new country, the United States. He had sent L'Enfant, a tall, dignified Frenchman, to design what would become Washington, D.C. Then, it was simply a large stretch of land donated by the new states of Maryland and Virginia.

Two years earlier, President Washington had decided that the new nation needed a permanent headquarters. He decided to move the country's headquarters from Philadelphia and New York City. He wanted a city built and designed for the capital. He picked the newly created District of Columbia, but the decision had not been easy. Many states wanted the federal government to move to their own areas. After much argument and debate, an agreement was reached. In the summer of 1790, President Washington signed a bill to locate the nation's capital in the District of Columbia.

Major L'Enfant knew that it would not be easy to turn this rugged land into a beautiful city. The United States did not have much money then. It would take many years of hard work, but he knew it could be done.

In Charleston, South Carolina, another man was about to become part of history. James Hoban, an Irish **architect**, worked by candlelight in the kitchen of his home. A prize of $500 was being offered to the person who could design the best house for the President. He knew he could win. He studied his architecture books. He looked at the plans stretched across his table. He asked his wife for her ideas. For weeks he worked on his plans for a gracious mansion. He knew it would have to be **elegant**, but he also knew that President Washington would not want it to look like a castle for a king.

Finally, his plans were finished. He looked at them one last time and he was satisfied that he had done his best work. He carefully wrapped the plans and sent them on the next stagecoach to the three **commissioners** in the new "Federal City."

James Hoban wasn't the only architect to enter the contest. Plans also came from eighteen other designers. When George Washington saw the plans drawn by James Hoban, however, he was very impressed. He studied them very carefully. He liked the large oval-shaped **reception** room that James Hoban had designed. Even though he decided to make some of the rooms smaller, President Washington chose James Hoban's plans. The original plans called for a large front porch. They also called for large wings, or additional rooms, on each side. President Washington decided that the front porch and the large wings would have to wait.

George Washington asked James Hoban to come to "Federal City" and supervise the building of the President's mansion. On October 12, 1792, James Hoban watched from a grassy hillside as the cornerstone for the President's house was laid. It was the first government building to be started on the 10 square mile tract of land.

He must have been a little discouraged. The workers had to fight the mosquitoes from the nearby swamps. Congress had very little money. Supplies and materials were hard to get and winter would soon arrive. Fortunately, President Washington did not plan to move the government to "Federal City" until 1800. Despite the delays, James Hoban thought the mansion could be built in eight years.

Work progressed very slowly. In June of 1800, the government began moving its offices to the District of Columbia. On November 1, 1800, John Adams, our second president,

The Oval Office as it looks today, after the recent redecoration by the Bush Administration.

moved into the mansion, even though it was not finished. His second night in the house, he wrote a letter to his wife, Abigail. In the letter, he wrote: "I pray Heaven to bestow the best of blessings on this house and all that shall hereafter inhabit it. May none but honest and wise men ever rule under this roof."

The White House was never completed

exactly the way James Hoban designed it. Each president has added to the many changes of the mansion. Several major changes have been made. For nearly 200 years, the White House has stood as a monument to the great vision of George Washington, Pierre Charles L'Enfant and James Hoban.

ABIGAIL ADAMS AND HER NEW HOME

Two weeks after her husband moved into the President's mansion, Abigail Adams arrived in "Federal City." At first, she was shocked by the unfinished rooms and the damp plaster. There was very little furniture and most of the rooms were empty. When she moved in, only six rooms could be used.

Mrs. Adams soon learned that the ground floor was for the work rooms and the servants quarters. The state rooms and reception areas were on the first floor. The President's office and his family's living quarters were on the second floor.

Even though she only lived there four months before the next president moved in, Abigail Adams did her best to make the house more comfortable. During the cold winter months, she had a hard time finding enough wood for the thirteen fireplaces. She did not have enough lamps to light all the rooms at night. Slowly, she got used to the mud from the men who continued to work on the rooms. She even had to hang her laundry in the large, unfinished East Room.

But Abigail Adams knew that someday the mansion would be completed. When it was, it would be a grand building, a perfect place for parties with kings and world leaders. In a letter to her daughter, she once wrote, "This house is built for the ages to come." Her hard work made her proud of the mansion. On New Year's Day 1801, she and her husband held a reception in the upstairs Oval Room. The fireplaces burned brightly and candles glowed in each of the rooms. Dressed in their red uniforms, the Marine Band played in the background.

In March of 1801, Thomas Jefferson, the new president, moved into the mansion. Thomas Jefferson was concerned about the name of this home. Many people called it the President's Palace. He thought that name was too formal. He asked that his home be called the President's House. He once described the house as "big enough for two emperors, one Pope and the grand lama."

THE PRESIDENT'S HOUSE AND ITS MANY FAMILIES

Thomas Jefferson wanted to make the President's House a more comfortable place to live, work, and conduct important business. He brought furniture from his home at Monticello in Virginia. He put some of his most elegant furniture in the State Oval Room. He used this room to greet special guests. Today it is called the Blue Room. It is considered one of the most beautiful rooms in the White House. Jefferson also added a porch and built terraces on the east and west sides of the house. These terraces included offices, stables and storage sheds. He never finished the East Room (where Mrs. Adams hung her laundry). Instead, he used it as an extra pantry.

Thomas Jefferson liked to hold parties at the President's House. He invited all kinds of important people including Indian chiefs. He also invited **common** workers and laborers. Many of these parties featured unusual foods cooked by his French chef.

Thomas Jefferson was not the only president who liked to have parties. Dolley Madison, the wife of the next president, James Madison, held many parties at the house. She even held a Easter party for all the children in Federal City. She dyed hundreds of eggs herself so the children could roll the eggs on the lawn of the President's House.

Congress gave Dolley Madison money to buy more furniture. She decorated many rooms with fine, elegant furniture. Unfortunately, the United States went to war against England in 1812. In 1814, the British marched on Washington. President Madison left to be with the troops. Mrs. Madison was alone at the President's House. By late summer she began to worry. On August 23, 1814 she wrote a letter to her sister. In the letter she said that she had filled her trunks with important government papers and loaded them in a carriage. She said the furniture could not be protected. The next day she wrote a second letter to her sister. She wrote that she could hear the sounds of the cannons. She did not want to leave without her husband. But on August 24, 1814, she was told that she had to sneak away. She dressed as a poor farmer's wife. She took a large painting of George Washington down from a wall. She broke the frame and rolled up the painting. She then quickly rode off in a waiting coach. If she had waited any longer, she might have been taken prisoner by the British.

That night, the British burned down the government buildings. By morning, the President's House and the elegant furniture were destroyed. All that was left were the outside walls. Those walls were burned and covered with black ash and soot. A small stream of smoke rose from the building.

Dolley Madison and her husband never came back to the President's House. Once again, James Hoban came back to the nation's capital. He was asked to help rebuild the President's home. It had to be completely rebuilt. The insides were destroyed. The blackened out side walls were painted white. It took nearly four years to rebuild. Congress spent all the money it could to rebuild the house. The cost was about $500,000. There was very little money left to buy new furniture. So when the next President, James Monroe, moved in, the house was nearly empty. The famous painting of George Washington, saved by Dolley Madison, was returned. Today it hangs in the East Room. James Monroe and his family used their own furniture from France to decorate the house. Some of their furniture is still in the White House today.

When the Monroes were settled in, they began inviting guests back to the President's House. Their parties included Wednesday night receptions. During these receptions, any citizen was welcome to visit with the President's family.

When Andrew Jackson became President in 1829, the White House went through several major changes. President Jackson finished decorating the East Room. **Chandeliers**, marble-topped tables and colorful drapes of blue and yellow were added. Water was finally piped into the building. And a porch, called a **portico**, was added on the north side of the President's House. Because of the portico, the President's House was given the official address of 1600 Pennsylvania Avenue. Today, the north entrance is used only for kings and very important guests.

President Jackson was born in a log cabin. He was one of the first "common" men elected president. Many of his friends were common backwoods people. His parties had a reputation for being noisy and rowdy. One rowdy party was held just before he left office. At this party he was given a huge round of cheese that weighed 1400 pounds. By the time the party was over, cheese was smeared everywhere. It took several weeks to clean up the mess.

Andrew Jackson had turned the East Room into a formal reception room. Other presidents' families did not always use it that way. It has been used as a roller skating rink. Bicycles have been ridden across its floors. It has been a game room. President Lincoln's son, Tad, kept a goat in that room. It was a bunk house for Union troops during the Civil War. John Quincy Adams used it as a guest room for his pet alligator. And it was Teddy Roosevelt's favorite spot for recreation and wrestling.

In the 1840s, gas lights were installed in the President's House. Actually, they were first installed in every room but the East

Today the East Room has a variety of uses, including special performances.

Room. President James Polk's wife preferred candles in the chandelier. The first bathtub was put in the President's House in the 1850s for President Millard Fillmore. Many people told him not to install the bathtub. At that time, bathing in a tub was actually con-sidered dangerous. He also had a cookstove placed in the kitchen. His cooks preferred fireplace cooking and complained. He eventually had to teach the cooks how to use the stove. When the Fillmore family moved

Many improvements have been made over the years to keep the White House beautiful.

in, Mrs. Fillmore was concerned that the President's House had no books. Soon the first books were also purchased.

By the end of the Civil War, the President's House was again in need of repairs. The rugs and curtains were worn to threads. The furniture was full of bugs and covered

22

with stains. In 1865, President Andrew Johnson's daughter had the house cleaned and had **slip covers** placed on the worn out furniture. In 1869, when Ulysses S. Grant moved in, the entire house was **renovated**. New furniture was purchased and the walls were covered with wallpaper.

An important moment in White House history took place on June 2, 1886. Grover Cleveland became the only President to ever be married in the White House. While President Cleveland was in office the hot-water heating system was replaced with a "modern" steam system. Electric lights also were added. Mrs. Cleveland began a collection of Presidential china. The collection is still on display today in the China Room on the ground floor.

Theodore Roosevelt arrived with his family in 1901. The President's House now faced a new problem. It had become too small. There was no longer enough room for the President's family and all his staff members. To make matters worse, engineers discovered that the house's foundation was becoming weak.

In 1902 Congress set aside $540,641 to repair the 100-year house. President Roosevelt moved his family out and carpenters, painters, steel workers and masons moved in. Steel beams were placed in the basement. The State Dining Room was enlarged so that it could seat one hundred people. More bedrooms and bathrooms were added. This allowed the second floor to become a private area for the President's family. A wing of offices was added for the President and his staff.

Another important change took place at that time. Until then, the President's home had been called the "President's House" and the "Executive Mansion." Many people had nicknamed it the "White House" because of its striking white outside walls. President Roosevelt decided it was time to make the new name official. In 1902 Congress passed a law giving it the official title of the White House.

It wasn't long before the President's staff and family once again outgrew the White House. President Calvin Coolidge had a third floor built. It included more bedrooms and storage areas. A swimming pool was built for President Franklin D. Roosevelt.

During Harry Truman's early years in office it appeared that the White House was ready to crumble. A story is told that during a reception in 1948, the East Room's chandelier began to sway back and forth. People also said they heard cracking sounds. The house was worn out and the foundation was cracking. The floors and walls could no longer take the stress. The White House would have to either be demolished or completely rebuilt. The Trumans moved across the street to the Blair House. Once they were gone, the bulldozers and work crews came.

The White House was considered an important symbol to the American people. Americans had learned to love the White House. They wanted it to continue to look the same. Because of this, the original four outside walls were left standing. But the inside was completely gutted. The White House simply became an empty shell, as it had been after the fire in 1814.

The White House was completely rebuilt from the inside out. The inside was carefully taken apart. Two new basements were dug. This gave the White House a total of five floors. A new steel framework was built inside the shell. Important parts of the house's trim also were taken apart. They were saved and reassembled when the construction was finished. The White House was rebuilt exactly to its original appearance. Only one staircase was changed. The total bill for the "new" White House was nearly $6,000,000.

In 1961, President John F. Kennedy and his family moved into the White House. His wife, Jackie, decided the furniture of the White House should continue to be restored. She wanted the White House to reflect the entire history of the U.S. Presidency and American life. She wanted the White House to become a national show place. She formed a committee. This committee helped obtain historic furniture and other items of interest.

INSIDE THE MODERN WHITE HOUSE

More than two million tourists visit the White House each year. They are able to take specially guided tours on Monday through Friday each week. The three main floors of the White House are the ground floor, the first floor, and the second floor. The first floor is also called the State Floor. It is an area of particular interest to the tourists who come from all over the United States and the world.

The largest room on the State Floor is the East Room. It is one of the first rooms that a visitor will see on a White House tour. It is decorated in white and gold. It is used as a grand reception for very special occasions. It has been used for plays, concerts and recitals. Beautiful chandeliers hang from the ceiling. Famous paintings of George Washington and Martha Washington hang on the walls. The East Room looks basically the same today as it did in 1902. It is such a beautiful room today that it is hard to believe an alligator, a goat, and Union soldiers have lived in it.

At the western end of the State Floor is the State Dining Room. This is the second largest room on the floor. More than one hundred people can be seated in this room. It is also decorated in white and gold. On one of the walls hangs a large painting of Abraham Lincoln. The State Dining Room has been the scene of many dinners for famous guests. James Hoban originally designed the room to be a "public" dining room.

The State Dining Room and the East Room are connected by the Main Hall. It is lighted by two cut-glass chandeliers. They were made more than two hundred years ago. A large red carpet runs through the Main Hall. Leading to the Main Hall is the Entrance Hall. It is at the floor's north end.

South of the Main Hall are the Red, Blue and Green rooms. The Green Room is next to the East Room. It has been used as a sitting room, or parlor, by many presidents. It is called the Green Room because it is decorated in shades of green. It was decorated in this color after the fire of 1814. Above the

The Main Hall

fireplace hangs a famous painting of Benjamin Franklin. It looks much the same as it did when Thomas Jefferson was president.

The Red Room is next to the State Dining Room. It has been used as a parlor by the First Lady and her guests. It is often used for special teas, informal gatherings, or after-dinner parties. Its walls are actually scarlet in color. Many important events have taken place in this room. In 1877, Inauguration Day fell on Sunday. So President-elect Rutherford B. Hayes was sworn in as President in this room on Saturday night. (The ceremony was repeated on Capitol Hill on Monday.) Portraits of several presidents hang on the walls. One of the paintings is a famous portrait of President Woodrow Wilson. It was painted in Paris, France, in 1919. Many of the First Ladies have had their portraits painted in this room.

In between the Red Room and the Green Room is the Blue Room. It is one of three oval-shaped rooms designed by James Hoban. He wanted it to be the central reception room in the President's house. The room is decorated in shades of white and blue. A large chandelier hangs from the middle of the ceiling. Three large windows allow visitors to view the President's Park. The President's Park is also called the South Grounds.

The State Floor is often called the ceremonial headquarters of our nation. Many important leaders, kings, and queens have been entertained in the rooms on this floor. Many business leaders, private citizens and young people also have been invited to visit the President here.

The ground floor is where much of the President's work takes place. Many important meetings are held in the rooms of this floor. Located on this floor is the Library, the Vermeil Room, and the China Room. Also on this floor are workrooms and the Diplomatic Reception Room. Attached to the ground floor are the East and West wings.

The Diplomatic Reception Room also is a large, oval-shaped room. This room is used as the entrance to the White House by the President and his family. The walls are covered with panoramic wallpaper. On the wallpaper are pictures of historic events. The pictures are called "Scenic America." The pictures were painted in 1834. The wallpaper has scenes of Niagara Falls, the Natural Bridge of Virginia, and Boston Harbor. There also are scenes of West Point and New York Bay.

The White House has an outdoor terrace often used for
entertaining guests. There is a wonderful view of the
surrounding city.

Franklin D. Roosevelt used the Diplomatic Reception Room for his famous "fireside chats." His "fireside chats" were radio broadcasts to the American public. The messages were about what was happening in the United States and the world. The messages were called "fireside chats" even though the room has no fireplace.

The West Wing was built in 1902. When it was completed, the President's office was moved into the wing. But soon there was no longer enough room. In 1909, the Oval Office was built. It has been the location of the President's office ever since. It is a large, oval-shaped room which looks out at the Rose Garden. It is furnished with White House furniture. Each President also brings some of his favorite items. President John F. Kennedy put his favorite rocking chair in the office. President Ronald Reagan placed a large jar of his favorite jelly beans on the desk.

The room has a fireplace and sofas. Several famous naval paintings hang above the fireplace. The office has French doors that open onto a colonnade. A colonnade is similar to a fancy patio or pavilion. The colonnade faces the Rose Garden. Many presidents have used this area and the Rose Garden for private walks. President Lyndon B. Johnson liked to talk with television and newspaper reporters while taking walks in the Rose Garden.

Near the Oval Office is the **Cabinet** Room. Some of the most important decisions in history have been made in this room. The President's Cabinet meets here. The President often meets with legislative leaders or

The Oval Office looked like this when Jimmy Carter was President. It was recently redecorated.

important groups in this room. The National Security Council meets in this room as well.

The International Situation Room also is located in the West Wing. In this room are electronic machines from the Central Intelligence Agency and the Department of Defense. The President's staff uses the machines to learn about foreign events.

The Cabinet Room.

There are maps used to keep track of the location of all our military forces. Many of the machines in this room are "classified." This means they are top secret.

Hundreds of newspaper, radio and television reporters work in Washington, D.C. They come from all over the United States and the world. Many are assigned to write stories about the activities of the President and his staff. Near the basement entrance to the White House offices is the White House Press Room. It is here that the reporters can write their stories.

Nearby is the White House Press Office. This is where the President's Press Secretary works. The Press Secretary often delivers messages or statements from the President to the press. He is often referred to as the Presidential Spokesperson. The Press Secretary has a large staff. The Press Office usually is very crowded.

The President and his family live on the second floor of the White House. In the President's living quarters are bedrooms, sitting rooms, a private dining room and a kitchen. The second floor has not always been used as a living area for the President's family. It has been used for offices, storage and meetings. As a result, many famous rooms can be found on this floor. Those rooms include the Lincoln Bedroom, the Treaty Room, and the Yellow Oval Room.

The Lincoln Bedroom was used as the Cabinet Room when Abraham Lincoln was President. It is now used as a guest room. One of the most important events in our nation's history took place in this room. On January 1, 1863, Lincoln sat in this room and signed the Emancipation Proclamation. In this room is a plaque which reads: "In this room Abraham Lincoln signed the Emancipation Proclamation of January 1, 1863 whereby four million slaves were given their freedom and slavery forever prohibited in these United States."

Across the hall is the Rose Guest Room. It also is called the Queens' Bedroom. Five Queens, including Queen Elizabeth of Great Britain, have stayed in this room. The room is decorated in shades of rose, red and white. The bedspread, canopy and curtains are covered with a rose pattern.

Down the hall is the Treaty Room. It was used as the President's Cabinet Room from just after the Civil War until the White House was rebuilt in 1902. A famous event

Reporters gathered on the portico, waiting to speak with
the President.

The Rose Garden.

also took place here. It was in this room that the treaty which ended the Spanish-American War was signed. Because of that, it was given its name.

Next to the Treaty Room is another large, oval-shaped room. It is called the Yellow Oval Drawing Room. It has been used as an office, a library and a private study. Today it is decorated in yellows and whites. It has a fireplace and comfortable sofas. Often, before important dinners, the leaders meet in this room. Presidents have met with many world leaders in the Drawing Room.

Outside the White House is the Rose Garden. It is next to the West Wing and the Oval Office. The first garden was planted for John Adams in 1800. Many presidents have added their favorite flowers and shrubs. John Quincy Adams planted tulips, York cabbages and peas. Andrew Jackson added magnolias. The first roses were planted in the garden in 1913 by Mrs. Woodrow Wilson. The garden is 125 by 90 feet in size.

The President's Park is the area within the fences around the White House. This area stretches from South Executive Avenue to Pennsylvania Avenue. Inside are fountains, walking paths and a tennis court. Many trees

from all over the United States are planted in the President's Park. They include American Elm, Northern Red Oak, Black Walnut, Japanese Maples and Magnolia Grandiflora. The President's Park is a very beautiful sight. In the spring, the flowers and trees bud and bloom in magnificent colors.

WASHINGTON, D.C. TODAY

George Washington and Pierre Charles L'Enfant would be proud to see what their "Federal City" has become today. James Hoban would also be proud to see the glistening White House on Pennsylvania Avenue. It has survived fires, wars and age. It has been the home of Presidents and their families. It has become a symbol of the United States.

Jenny had reached the last page of her picture book. She took one very last look at the large photograph of the White House. "I wonder what it would be like to live there," she thought.

GLOSSARY

ARCHITECT — A person whose profession is designing buildings, drawing up plans and supervising construction.

CABINET — The people who advise the President.

CHANDELIER — A light fixture which has several branches that hold candles or bulbs, usually hanging from the ceiling.

COMMISSIONER — A person authorized to perform certain duties or tasks.

COMMON — Ordinary, having characteristics shared by everyone.

ELEGANT — Graceful and dignified, as in dress and style; tasteful.

PORTICO — A porch or covered walk consisting of a roof supported by columns.

RECEPTION — A social event, usually formal, for the receiving of guests.

RENOVATED — To make new, to replace broken and worn parts.

SLIP COVER — A removable, fitted cover for furniture.